WILLOWS IN THE BREEZE

WILLOWS IN THE BREEZE

Enjoying God through Christian Verse

FELIX H. SENNITT

RESOURCE *Publications* • Eugene, Oregon

WILLOWS IN THE BREEZE
Enjoying God through Christian Verse

Copyright © 2021 Felix H. Sennitt. All rights reserved. Except for brief quotations in critical publications or reviews, no part of this book may be reproduced in any manner without prior written permission from the publisher. Write: Permissions, Wipf and Stock Publishers, 199 W. 8th Ave., Suite 3, Eugene, OR 97401.

Resource Publications
An Imprint of Wipf and Stock Publishers
199 W. 8th Ave., Suite 3
Eugene, OR 97401

www.wipfandstock.com

PAPERBACK ISBN: 978-1-7252-8490-6
HARDCOVER ISBN: 978-1-7252-8491-3
EBOOK ISBN: 978-1-7252-8492-0

03/31/21

CONTENTS

Introduction | vii
How? | 1
Avital | 2
He Sought | 4
Shame | 5
Sojourner | 7
Vine | 8
Honey | 9
A Whisper | 10
Temple | 11
Meditation | 12
Pins, Hooks, & Pegs | 13
And? | 14
Gift | 15
Olive Tree | 16
Hiding & Worshipping | 17
Riddle | 18
Clean & Unclean | 19
Shuffling Along | 20
Jubilee | 21
Throwing | 22
Silver | 24
Wings | 25
Heart & Frankincense | 26
Disciple | 27
He Found | 28
Veil | 29
Pleasant | 30
Guided to Water | 31
Treasured Possession | 32

Sapphire | 33
Eternity | 35
Dainty | 36
He Prayed | 37
Incomprehensibly Amazing | 38
Willow | 39
Righteousness | 40
Draw Near | 42
Small & Insignificant | 43
My Shepherd! | 45
Luxuriantly Fresh | 46
Lattice and Snow | 48
Meditation & Whisper | 50
Instruction | 51
Tambourine | 52
Suggested Bibliography | 53

INTRODUCTION

When I was in elementary school in 1987, I was told I had a 'rare' ability to write poetic verse. I loved playing with words back then, hearing their sounds, rolling them around in my mouth, and understanding their meanings. I still do. To this day I still learn new words. Words are so important because they convey meaning and emotions, not merely instructions and information. They unite souls and hearts, to nurture and love them – and also have the capacity to bruise and destroy. Back when I was seven, I was dissuaded from writing poetry because I was told it would 'not make money', as if that were the most important thing in life. So I stopped writing verse and fiction, even though I was good at writing them. But in 2018, I read a book on how to write poetry and eventually resumed the discipline of creating it. I have also started learning other languages, including Hebrew, Korean, and Norwegian, not necessarily because they serve a crudely functional purpose, but simply because I love language and words.

Then in 2020 I wrote a Masters of Theology thesis about the Bible and how writing poetry helps people to process grief. While doing this, and much to my amazement, I discovered that the Bible is filled with poetic words. Psalm 34 is written as an alphabetic acrostic poem, where the first word of each line begins with each successive letter of the Hebrew alphabet. Prophecy is written in poetry (Jeremiah 2:13). The Mosaic law of retribution in Leviticus 24:19–21 is written in a poetic structure, and approximately 85% of the book of Lamentations is an acrostic poem as it records the historical events of Jerusalem's destruction. Human experience is often written evocatively this way in Scripture:

> "See, Yahweh, for I am distressed:
> *my stomach is boiling*;
> *my heart is writhing*" (Lamentations 1:20, my own translation).[1]

Even eschatological truth is written poetic imagery: "As for the *likeness* of the living creatures, their appearance was *like* burning coals of fire, *like* the appearance of torches . . ." (Ezekiel 1:13a, NKJV, emphasis added). Jesus spoke poetically in Luke 9:58: "Foxes have holes and birds of the air have nests, but the Son of Man has nowhere to lay His head."

---

1. The writer does not just name an emotion; he paints a word picture with it using poetic imagery.

Throughout history, many Christians have been successful poets. George Herbert, Mary Sidney Pembroke, and John Donne, on whose shoulders I stand, come to mind. These individuals were friends of William Shakespeare and they are still quoted today in texts written by non-believers about how to write poetry. The Countess of Pembroke committed the entire book of Psalms to poetic meter in order to make God's word more accessible to her generation. Along with George Herbert, a pastor who only lived a brief existence on this earth, she also pioneered unique forms of writing verse – and without their collective contribution, modern English poetry would not be what it is today.

So why is it that I have written a book of poetry? When I wrote the verse contained in this book in 2019–2020, I was not writing them for publication. I was writing them more for my own personal enjoyment than anything else. But then I realized that there was a need for poetry in the wider world, particularly verse about God and His goodness. This is so necessary because our world today lacks a) an appreciation of God and His glory; and b) a loving, careful, and edifying use of words. Words today are thrown around like hand grenades to attack people, ruin societies, to manipulate, to register offence, and to complain. Words like 'he' and 'she' are being re-defined so that they no longer mean what they were originally defined as. Marriage is no longer strictly defined as being between a man and a woman by many legislatures, which causes confusion – and destruction. And where confusion is there will be chaos.

Yet when the poetry this contained in this book was written, I simply wanted to bring some grace and order to all this ugly chaos; I wanted to do this by marrying beautiful, poetic words with the glory of God. I have done this primarily with reference to how God has worked in my own life (e.g. *Small and Insignificant*); the current global health crisis (*And?*); as well as marveling at the beauty of God (e.g. *Sapphire*). Having said this, it may seem like much of this verse concerns myself; admittedly, much poetry can be like this and when it is done badly, it sounds self-centered, pretentious, and dull. However, although there are biographical elements to my verse they have been written with the intention not only of glorifying God in the process, but to encourage you, the reader, to do the very same thing in your own unique circumstances. I even hope it will encourage you, God willing, to take up poetry writing yourself.

To enjoy the full impact of the verses contained in this book, it is highly recommended that you read the poems aloud, when and where you can. This helps with sounding things out and makes them more memorable. I have tried to make the rhyming schemes to work, but in many cases it may not. Being an Australian myself, these poems were written with an

Australian accent in mind, although efforts were made to ensure that the rhyming scheme worked in any accent. If it does not, then I apologize: it was completely unintentional.

The poems have also been written according to various lengths and according to different structures so as to avoid the verse becoming predictable and, therefore, boring. This volume contains an Alexandrine; various pantoums; a ghazal; some kyrielles; and a number of Vietnamese lục bát. If you have no idea of what I am referring to, that doesn't matter. But if you are a poetry buff, you will notice them.

As for *how* I wrote these poems into being, that is a story in itself. At seminary, I learned Hebrew – and it is a language that I have come to love, like an old friend. Its alphabet contains 22 letters, and as I learned Hebrew I picked up some of its words. *Avital*, for instance, means 'My Father is Dew' (from 2 Sam. 3:4). *Bosh* means shame, and so on. So I went through this Hebraic alphabet from A to Z (or 'Aleph to Taw, to be precise) and chose a word that began with each letter. Then I used that letter as a theme for each poem. In some of the poems I have actually incorporated the Hebraic word into the poem: for instance, you will see the word 'gair' in the fifteenth line of the poem *Sojourner*. These words have been italicized. Included below is a table which outlines all the words that I chose for the theme of each poem. The poems, as you may notice, reflect the meaning of the Hebraic word around which the poems were written. If this does not make sense to you now, do not worry. You will eventually see it as you read on.

Hebrew Letter	Hebrew Word	Poem Title
א	*aikah* *avital*	How? My Father is Dew
ב	*baqash* *bosh*	He Sought Shame
ג	*gair* *gefen*	Sojourner Vine
ד	*davash* *damamah*	Honey A Whisper
ה	*heycal* *hegyon*	Temple Meditation
ו	*vav* *V'*	Pins, Hooks, & Pegs And?
ז	*zeved* *zayit*	Gift Olive Tree
ח	*chava(h)* *chidah*	Hiding & Worshipping Riddle

ט	tamay(ah) tafaf	Clean & Unclean Shuffling Along
י	yovel yarah	Jubilee Throwing
כ	ceseph canaf	Silver Wings
ל	lavav, levonah limud	Heart & Frankincense Disciple
מ	matza' masaveh	He Found Veil
נ	no'eem nahal	Pleasant Guided to Water
ס	segulah saffir	Treasured Possession Sapphire
ע	'olam 'anog	Eternity Dainty
פ	palal pilee	He Prayed Incomprehensibly Amazing
צ	tsaf-fsafah tzedekah	Willow Righteousness
ק	qarav qaton	Draw Near Small & Insignificant
ר	ro-ay ra'anan	My Shepherd! Luxuriantly Fresh
שׁ שׂ	S'vacah, sheleg sichah shametz	Lattice & Snow Meditation & Whisper
ת	torah tof	Instruction Tambourine

At the end of this book I have included a very brief bibliography of suggested books if you are interested in knowing more about poetry.

Now that you know a bit about me and how this book came to existence, I now commend its verse to you for edification and encouragement. If you are not a Christian reading it, I pray that it brings you to a saving knowledge and appreciation of our Lord and Savior Jesus Christ, so that you will find your salvation in Him and Him alone.

To God be the glory,
Felix Sennitt.

HOW?

The deepest question I dared to ask 1
Was when I walked down the footpath.
Concern had creased my furrowed brow:
I begged to know the why and how.

Must the aged get old and baggy? 5
Must I be teased for dressing daggy?
To know all things I took a vow:
I begged to know the why and how.

Why do the priests look so devout
And children like to scream and shout? 10
Alas, how? Tell me right now!
I begged to know the why and how.

Why need peacocks colorfully strut
And all the dads earn sagging guts?
Make a purse from the ears of sows? 15
I begged to know the why and how.

Yet all the queries never told me
Why my mother died so quickly.
Perhaps one day God will allow
For me to know the why and how. 20

AVITAL

The desert sands are twisting, parched
And just for rain they lie in wait
For billows black to fall, descend
To bathe under torrential cover.
Red hungry rocks reach out for dew,   5
Their hardened throats quite hard to quench.

Seeds entombed in soil sit unquenched
In tortured, passive time. Dry, parched,
Anticipating moisture, dew,
Under dark onerous cover   10
They so patiently sleep and wait.
In time, their life-flow shall descend.

Lightening fights water to descend
To supply minerals to quench
Nature's need, open and covered.   15
The blood of Christ feeds men's souls parched
From weight of sin and groaning wait.
In times due the Jews drank God's dew.

In my soul pours my Father's dew;
Down to me my Father descends   20
Caring to end a lonely wait.
I reach for Him, His grace to quench
What selfishness made worn and parched.
Droplets adorn my head's cover.

Love like this is my sin's cover— 25
The Son's rich blood is rich with dew.
No soil so red is quite as parched
As those who, in sin, did descend;
The tongues of restless souls unquenched
Have need no more to writhe and wait. 30

The pure white chorus now awaits
Where Father's mantle shall cover
My resurrected body quenched.
Avital: My Father is Dew
Is the name for Him who descends, 35
Who waters us no more be parched.

Envoi
High Father, I await Your dew;
Cover me as Your love descends.
Quench my spirit so dry and parched.

HE SOUGHT

Up to the blue the dog held high
To track down where the scent did lie:
Down he bent in a desperate walk
To get the prize his frenzy sought.

No stone remained for his nostrils 5
Rock cold and wet in his tussles.
All bursts to block him came to nought
To get the prize his frenzy sought.

His mind returned to puppy days
When then he learned to hunt small prey 10
Like all the tennis balls he caught
And got the prize his frenzy sought.

At last the hunting all paid off,
As sweetened taste outweighed the rough.
His yelp descried, "I'll not stop short 15
To get the prize my frenzy sought!"

Off the track I once turned out lost
And Christ, to find me, paid the cost.
By His dear blood my soul was bought
To get the prize His frenzy sought. 20

SHAME

That fear which feared to speak his name
Hid quaking tense inside a fridge.
That frozen scared, embarrassed Shame
Would not traverse the open ridge.

Hid quaking tense inside a fridge   5
No loving smile could coax Shame out;
None could traverse the open ridge
To find Shame at his exiled mount.

No loving smile could coax Shame out:
He thought that frost might scald his bones. 10
To find Shame at his exiled mount
You sought one frightened and alone.

Shame thought that frost might scald his bones
Yet yearned for understanding ears;   15
You sought one frightened and alone.
Why not? Disgrace had singed his years.

Yearning for understanding ears
He oft withdrew when love came close.
Why not? Disgrace had singed his years, 20
And buried hope which he had lost.

He oft withdrew when love came close
But then one day he came to me,
The buried hope which he had lost
Revitalized at being set free.   25

On that one day he came to me
I heard all that he had to say;
Revitalized at being set free
He wept and even laughed to play.

I heard all that he had to say;   30
That frozen scared, embarrassed Shame.
He wept and even laughed to play,
Who once had feared to speak his name.

SOJOURNER

In thickened boots we trudged the slopes
In valleyed fear and heightened hopes,
To feel the wind inside our hair
In sojourn to where lights burn fair.

Forest glades I wanted to take;
For you a rippling, glassy lake
And all of nature to compare,
In sojourn to where lights burn fair.

The sleet hit hard to slow our pace
And scorched the joy off your dear face;
We survived cursed rocky stairs
In sojourn to where lights burn fair.

At night some possums pinched our food
And spoiled our winsome, cheeky mood
When what you sought (you weary *gair*)
Was to sojourn where lights burn fair.

Well, here we are in Heaven's arms
Far from devilled arrows and harms.
Behold our Lamb with golden hair,
Our sojourn's goal where lights burn fair.

VINE

Greens from the vine crunch solemn, sweet
When troubles come with me to meet.
On sweaty days of summer hot
The vines bear fruit for salad pots,
Or spew some wine 'fore human feet.					5

When sunlight and green grapes do greet
The darkness fades to joy replete
With graceful blooms of promise. What
      Greens from the vine!

Reddened grapes have to stand the heat			10
Of disappointing, sad defeat
Of having what green grapes have not:
Boring taste and suspicious spots.
With deep respect I will so treat
      Greens from the vine.					15

HONEY

Milky clouds sent south my zest
To milk the joy from my warm breast:
My daily dreams now badly scuppered;
I craved some honey for my supper.

My damsel's body ached with pain; 5
Our money soon went down the drain.
Our girls from bullies there to suffer . . .
I craved some honey for my supper.

I strained to fight cosmic battles.
Allies betrayed, which left me baffled. 10
I groaned, "Come on, you silly duffer!
Let's get some honey for our supper."

Deep within her yellowed syrup
That sweet nectar spurred my stirrups
And up I jumped with laughter 15
To get more honey for my supper.

With His embrace my Jesus feeds me
With golden love that rocks me sleepy
For deep He gives me like no other:
His cares I crave for my supper. 20

A WHISPER

In a whisper love slowly grows
And what one thinks one only knows.
In squeaking voice lines just eke out
For some to hear but never shout.
Such private worlds bypass the nose.

Tyrants of strength cannot out-tow
Men's private thoughts at volumes low.
The thinker throws his power about
In a whisper.

God in His might to paces slow
Elects to speak. Yes, it is so.
Men look to thunder for His mouth
But He speaks in decibels south.
We only get what He will blow
In a whisper.

TEMPLE

On Sundays are our markets full
Where men bow down to sales on wool
And sell their souls for prices slipped:
What shall be our place of worship?

Once I served in the House of Lust   5
With perversions that died in dust
In soul and body all outstripped:
What shall be our place of worship?

Each day our eyes are glued to screens
In trembling awe of things unseen   10
Heeding the priest of Youtube clips.
What shall be our place of worship?

In Jesus Christ the Temple walked
Whipping tables as Satan baulked!
He arose days later after He chipped.   15
What shall be our place of worship?

Christ the Temple stands firm to last;
In us a temple die is cast
With God's Spirit making us fit
To enter His place of worship.   20

MEDITATION

This jumbled mix inside my heart
Pairs sweet with foul just for a start.
Light and thoughts worth condemnation
Fill each day my meditation
And in between grey, murky parts. 5

From each these stems I do impart
Life or death when folk cross my path.
I give, at God's invitation
This jumbled mix.

Dead thoughts must stop as baby sparks, 10
Lest they give birth and trouble starts.
Attitudes worth abnegation,
Inner vows, insinuation,
Be overcome so sin departs
This jumbled mix. 15

PINS, HOOKS, & PEGS

At the country manor oaken
Doors creaked inwards, slightly broken
As opulent rugs graced my feet
Where pins, hooks, and pegs hang replete.

King's portraits stood from floor to ceiling 5
Infusing me with regal feeling.
From their battles I felt their heat
Where pins, hooks, and pegs hang replete.

Erect and proud these ancient folk
Steeled themselves through hard battle strokes 10
Then stood their ground with iron feet
Where pins, hooks, and pegs hang replete.

Embroidered tapestries do cover
Tables where queens dined with brothers.
Now we snack there on biscuits sweet 15
Where pins, hooks, and pegs hang replete.

The fits of life give me no hassles:
A hook of gold on Yahweh's tassels
Am I, as had these tables neat
Where pins, hooks, and pegs hang replete. 20

AND?

Awaking bright with crud-stained face
News of lethal virus breaks:
Noxious virus (it's Chinese)
Drags the world down to its knees.

I shake my shoulders, wondering, "And?" 5
Will the world much longer stand?"
Fear is rife in every street.
Smiles meet no more when strangers greet.

Toilet paper holds them tight,
Comfort hugged throughout the night. 10
A love is forged more than desire:
One's spouse is hand sanitizer.

The lockdown panic burns the ears
Cutting hope from youthful years.
None shall gain on me control 15
For Jesus saves my body, soul.

Heaven be my home at death:
This world is not my feathered nest.
If, to nought, come all my plans
I'll shrug my shoulders, asking, "And?" 20

GIFT

He came home tired, lathered in sweat
Sweetened with scents that pine trees get,
Weary from chopping forests all day
With dollars, not gifts, for his pay.

The nurse, his wife, banked her cheque   5
For rounding off her patient checks,
And cleaning vomit stains away
With dollars, not gifts, for her pay.

Scruffy and barking their canine
Lay down in dirt at the clothes line;   10
He was paid for keeping pests at bay
With biscuits, not gifts, for his pay.

A gift, not pay—something for free?
It's not something we often see.
'Earn your worth' is our measure today   15
In dollars, not gifts, for our pay.

Yet Jesus, on Calvary's tree,
Gave gifts for our delivery.
Our wages were death, which kept God away
Yet bled His gift to dock sin's pay.   20

OLIVE TREE

The bubbling squawks of loud schoolyard noise
In afternoons of sweet blissful thinking
Explode from lungs of tired girls and boys
While sunsets begin descent to sinking.

Lawn grass is cut with lawn mowers lunging 5
In greedy lust to amputate growth;
Vegetation with voices plunging
Release their scents of freshly cut hope.

Clothes white and colored strung out to dry
Give mothers some jobs to keep them busy; 10
Online, the films give them cause to cry
And giggle their hair from straight to frizzy.

Site construction scaffolds city landscapes
Providing solid frames for the pulse
Beats for our civilisation to scrape 15
From day to day, for the true and false.

How blessed are we with rich, fruitful bowls
Of western affluence overflowing.
How long shall these our olive trees hold,
Producing sustenance richly flowing? 20

HIDING & WORSHIPPING

My garden walk saw me hemmed in:
At first I paced in trusting bliss
But then I covered up with sin
Not far from where the serpent hissed.
In me so much was now amiss.   5
His face was stern now I'd hidden
And much was feared when I was bidden.

When He saw me in such a state
His gazed pierced through my slender frame;
To run away I couldn't wait   10
And throw at others shards of blame.
Could I bow to the Holy Name?
In fleeting moments this I sought
But worship was a 'must' and 'ought'.

Since that time Jesus' blood has cleansed   15
White my soul—and boldly I come
Worshipping with family and friend.
The veil removed, my freedom won!
Where to hide apart from the Son?
My shame now flung into the sea,   20
I worship with a heart set free.

RIDDLE

Cats have secretaries; dogs have masters
And octopi fit through tiny, small holes.
Why stick wallpaper over the plaster?

Why do kids rebel when they leave the fold?
How does age reduce strong men to dribble?　　　5
Why doubt Scripture where the future is told?

Twisting and turning are these, life's riddles:
When you look for something you won't find it;
When you seek not it's bang in the middle.

Your muscles die when, for hours, you sit;　　　10
Try to be happy, joy may soon escape;
Live for comfort, your soul goes to the Pit.

Limp and sour tasted the crunchy grapes;
Accidentally you did some inventing;
You managed somehow to get out of a scrape.　　　15

I cannot say why life is so vexing,
Riddlesome, enigmatic, . . . and perplexing.

CLEAN & UNCLEAN

The drive to town at first was smooth
And all onboard had washed their skin,
But then a smell began to ooze:
Upon hot air it chose to swim
And fill our nostrils to the brim. 5
Hard it was to know what to do
And be rid of that doggy do.

Upon my daughter's sole it gripped—
Though it was only a smidgen;
So hard it was to get it nipped 10
Like gooey mess from filthy pigeons.
We needed expert opinion.
Such a tiny dollop of waste
Could damage much in tiny space.

'Fore our Maker's presence we stand; 15
Our sins, though small, stench us unclean.
From His face we are banished, banned.
Yet Righteous Christ can wash us clean,
Scrubbing us through: a prince's dream!
Now we can walk in blood-stained white, 20
Looking like our Saviour Light.

SHUFFLING ALONG

In the shuffling and bustling of busyness fast
There's so much we don't see as the present blows past.
Romping quickly to habit familiar inside
It's so hard just to know if the government's lied,
If the work of our toil makes just one little blotch,   5
If the meeting arranged is the best for the clock.
Do the shuffle down George Street to Circular Quay,[1]
Or express to the bathroom just to pee.
What the Dickens does dust-kicking do for our lot
When the good which we want helps forget what we've got?   10
In our hugs go our notes with our eyes to the ground
And with jackhammers blasting we hear not a sound.
All this civilisation ('progressive' it's called)
Must eventually come to a shuffling cold stall.

---

1. *George Street is the main road which runs right through Sydney's central business district (CDB). Circular Quay is the ferry terminal at the end of George Street, and is situated between the Harbour Bridge and the Sydney Opera House.*

JUBILEE

Her heavy back ached from an icy grip
With debts she had, old and outstanding.
Upon her shoulders were heavy chips
Though, to others, she was in fine standing.
From her debts the Father ached to free her: 5
Her body racked sore from toe to finger.

Around, around she circled through wild sands
Then came to Jesus' wooden Yom Kippur;
Her debts now cancelled by His bleeding hands,
A queen she became by the King made poor. 10
His grace beckoned her heart, "Open the door!
Release your scars to Me to come bind them,
Then you may set free others from ransom!"

Collapsing in a heap she welled up tears
In heatbreaking pain rememb'ring old wounds 15
Of scalding mem'ries and mummified fears.
The grip on her back died in a vacuum,
And her heart warmed a fire for love to bloom.
The cross of dear Christ at cold Calvary
Enabled for Rose her own Jubilee. 20

THROWING

In pride he stood so tall with strength erect,
A muscled frame designed to steal your breath.
With golden letters written on his head
The words The Law blazed on helmet lead.

"The Truth," said he with his olive-tanned grin   5
"Is in my hand to throw with hasty spin.
My javelin's ready to strike at your chest:
Your best preparation is sin confessed!"

This agent of God pierced right through my bowels
And it hurt so much I had to lie down: 10
He'd exposed things rebellious and wicked
Though this surgery was just the ticket.

It ached like Hades and I could not stand
Yet Law never stooped to lend me a hand.
Bruised, crushed, and battered, I rolled to one side   15
And wished at that moment that I had died.

Yet in that moment came a friend named Grace
With a love brightly shining from His face.
"Law can't save you, but he smashed Me for you.
I obeyed the laws which you couldn't do,"   20

Said He with a smile as He stroked my frame;
From that moment on I was never the same.
Infused with His light, shot like an arrow,
Truth surged throughout, right down to my marrow.

The Spear Master, Law, can no more condemn 25
Though Grace helps me keep the commands he sends.
My Righteousness, Christ, helps me here and now
To be holy when I do not know how.

SILVER

Within our crust of sandy brown
Wild reddish forces in anger rage;
The bold sun burns against the ground
And sees himself so wise and sage,
To cook us crisp atop earth's stage.　　　　　　　5
Breaking forth in hopeful quiver
Are glistening puffs of cloudy silver.

Golden lustres warm like butter
With a value beyond compare;
Yet yellow hues heat to smother,　　　　　　　10
To bend the head beneath the hair.
At shimmering white our eyes will stare
At circlets worn of rounded rivers,
Hand-made alone with cooling silver.

In lands so parched of liquid soul,　　　　　　　15
With broken cracks of throaty lines
We crave to have our hearts made whole
When light pours down and breaks through time,
For grapes to grow upon the vine.
There we will see darling slivers　　　　　　　20
Of gentle deep, and flowing silvers.

WINGS

Outside the gates grey light
Burning pale, dark as night, surrounds
As duty calls with sounds
Of rushing streams and hounds for prey.
Cold wind blows through the day 5
Although the roses play their game
As if they're owed great fame.
Misunderstanding came—I felt
Grief as the rain did pelt,
Of the scars I'd been dealt long past. 10
Will the tears always last?
Where the die has been cast I ache
As if my heart would break.
My life is no mistake: God sings
Over me where His wings 15
Cover deep, icy things. Father
Cares when dad would rather
Dive in jobs and harder cold toil.
May I never recoil
From those wings which toil to heal 20
What I've wrapped in a seal.
Over work or a meal His arms
Everlastingly calm
My storms in gentle palms so bright.

HEART & FRANKINCENSE

The wild cold blast of mean July[2]
Kept me indoors before a fire;
All rugged up, my clothes bone dry
And frankincense of silent choir
After days bogged down in squalid mire.　　　　　5
Glowing embers against black space
Warmed my chilled heart down from my face.

Those licking flames of God's warm breast
Dried the tendrils of strangling doubts;
And my head rested on His chest　　　　　　　　10
As He absorbed my aching shouts
Then gave me things to laugh about.
His loving arms, what frankincense!
What succor when no thing made sense.

The hardened contours of my face　　　　　　　　15
Faded out with a restored youth;
I danced before that fireplace
As burning pine did spark and shoot.
God's milky love had healed the roots.
What frankincense to fill my heart,　　　　　　　　20
A blazing fire out from a spark.

---

2. *In Australia, winter spans from June to August.*

DISCIPLE

The fifteen year old me
Sought no more suns to see and cried:
My hope within had died.
Cancer caused mom to slide and dad ...
Things went from stressed to bad;　　　　　　　　5
He frowned forever mad. Downcast,
In school chapel, I cast
My sorrows to the mast where God
Heard my tears as I sobbed
And never thought me odd. In pain　　　　　　　10
He made me His to gain
A disciple, the same as Christ,
A man of sorrow sight
And grief to bring God's light down here.
Once discipled by fears　　　　　　　　　　　　15
Death cannot cut not years. I'm free.

HE FOUND

Sprinting quickly on the double
Frantic frilled-necked lizards
Pass dire straits of deathly trouble,
To keep their juicy gizzards
From entering eagles' innards.   5
No other truth would dare resound
That in no way were they to be found.

Under stairs a boy surrounded
By sporting goods, feeling safe
Away from where anger sounded,   10
Where dread-filled sorrow burned and chafed.
He had no friends; he had no mates.
Lying below concrete ground,
He wished to curl up and not be found.

One day the Savior sought him   15
Out, to bring him to the light;
The boy followed reluctant, grim
In doubt. Was he a dreadful sight?
Christ showed no qualms, not even slight.
Jesus draped His warm arm around   20
The boy who, at last, was found.

VEIL

Delicately woven, dyed were fine veils
Draped over my brows, those serpentine veils.

A brazen lust for men suffocated
With loud opinion, the red opined veil.

Bitter resentment mummified love's reach:
I never noticed shame's oily, primed veil.

Pride's sophisticated gold, refined cloth
Shrouded my soul in the Devil's slimed vale.

Dazed, I shivered in that dark mine exposed
'Till Jesus peeled off those blinds and veils.

Those layers stripped bare, I could breathe again.
'Till Felix dies, He'll burn these maligned veils.

PLEASANT

Brightly sparkled anchors read
Of deaths brand new, etcetera,
Of sexploits of celebrities
And when tax men will getcha.
Did the magnate drown? You betcha. 5
Good news is like herding pheasant:
It's hard to find something pleasant.

Inhaling silver from the mist
My chest breathed airs of Heaven
When the fog my morning kissed 10
To purge me of sin's leaven,
To worship with the brethren.
The setting sun then kissed delight
To rock me warm unto the night.

The gorgeous and the turgid meet 15
Together in our fallen world.
Praise God, one day, they'll no more greet
When Satan's thrown down, hurled,
And dying is no more a word.
Then blizzard snows shall warm me white 20
In the Land of no more night.

GUIDED TO WATER

Over and over and over on I trekked
Bent down with burdens weighed on my neck
With marble cold, unliving.
I: unforgiving,
Worn from cares,   5
Sleep
Tortured dreams.
Next day howling screams
Desist as Jesus shoulders
My burdens and takes me to waters   10
Where The Shepherd feeds me with tanned, caring hands.

TREASURED POSSESSION

Sighing worn inside his breakfast chair
McGregor pushed aside his golden bowl
To slumber on the fifth floor of his lair,

The rooftop where he'd swim in pool waters
Cascading down rocks with oceanfront views.   5
Luxury oozed through every small quarter.

Devoid of one with whom to share his wealth
McGregor held his unwrinkled hands gently
Around his treasured possession. By stealth

The palm-sized chip of sapphire had smuggled   10
Its way inside its owner's warm embrace,
Reminding him to bring to Christ all his troubles.

SAPPHIRE

The sapphire throne
Stood bold, unflinching, unabashed, free
Blue gem convulsing like the writhing sea.
Cold touch under my feet, the blue path shimmered;
In my sky blue eyes that seat did glimmer.   5
My mind was blown.

I, overthrown,
Beheld unmatching, majestic red flame
To match the glory of Yahweh whose fame
Was sung amid a chorus angelic   10
Raising my heart to realms atmospheric,
Just me alone.

Such splendor known
In secret vision sees Father Yahweh
Trek with lighteninged feet all the night and day.   15
A perfume holy infused fleshly chests
And saints of time slept resting in His breast
With worship tones.

Men fully grown
Fell faceward down in broken strength and pride   20
With just themselves and nothing else to hide.
"We are undone!," we bellowed loudly out;
Every creature knew what we talked about.
Trumpets were blown!

A man unshown   25
Stood right beside the right-hand sapphire arm,
God's regent who had suffered sinners' harm.
He bid us all to come to kiss His hand
And find a refuge in the Great I Am.
What love was shown   30

When in that zone
Rushed billions to that hand to mercy find,
And there He smiled at me so patient, kind.
I wept as all my fears just fell apart
As liquid love filled up my hollow heart   35
Beside that throne.

Once guilty prone
From all my sinful, proud delight in lust,
I found that day they all had turned to dust.
Grace won that moment right when mercy poured   40
And there I fell down right down to the floor.
Now home
Is that sapphire throne.

ETERNITY

They said all good things must come to an end
And, burdened, their meaning came into light.
The last bite of warm pizza did portend

That, indeed, on all things sunsets will surely
Descend, with all dogs to have their last days.　　　5
The handcuffs of time do treat us poorly.

Our hearts yearn for eternity, *'olam*,
To let holidays endlessly rest our
Bodies serene, and work to keep its charm.

Eternity will amputate our tears,　　　10
And death's turgid breath will exhale no more,
For us to reign with Abba God from mansion tiers.

DAINTY

Delicate, refined
Small baby fingers stoke old wrinkled face,
The palm tree fronds massage warm windy place.
On souls of hard-worked hands a spouse's kiss
Soften hearts of hardness where love missed   5
Where life is unkind.

On beds to unwind,
A dark, secret pine forest in eras
Of stress when others refuse to hear us . . .
These impart their blessings when life gets tough,   10
When all we cry out is, "Enough! Enough!"
Anger to unbind

To Lord Jesus, kind,
In His tender, delicate mercies here
Who bears rage, frustrations, and lonely fears.   15
Where else to go except to Him who bore
Each our bruises as with His own before?
Here our rest we find.

HE PRAYED

The stained-glass edifice permeated
Saintly hues, where holy Scripture
Honeyed the dew, new life recreated.

Yet for all its biblical, muscled clout
My soul remained clamped by liturgical chants,   5
Unable to offer my murmured shouts.

To know the structure and vernacular
To give expression of my heart's desires!
Where could I learn this heavenly grammar?

The psalted breath of God's Holy Spirit   10
Gave me Jesus' words and Korah's dirges,
My tongue an incense for Heaven's throne to hear it.

INCOMPREHENSIBLY AMAZING

Giraffes at the zoo guzzled leaves; cows blew moo;
Elephants looked like Horton with Who.
"Wow!" we gawped; our cameras clicked
Who now sees those pics?
Already   5
We
Have seen sparks,
And amusement parks.
Yet incomprehensible,
Love ran down me bleeding sensible,   10
The crimson grace of Jesus for I and you.

WILLOW

By the rivers of Babylon, our own
Oceanic Babylon of comforts,
We sleep easy in the world we've made home.

I once played upon the harp delighted
To share in all the fruits of slumbering   5
Before life's emptiness had me frightened.

From the winds of life's aggressive billows
I ran to shimmering lime-green comfort,
The warm breezy calm of Jesus' willow.

Beneath this willow's thronging fringes we drop   10
Tears of heightened hope forlornly hung,
Praying, "Father, bring our worldly loves to a stop."

RIGHTEOUSNESS

This world's pollution reeks out;
A few know what it's about:
Dark smoke is not the dirt
Into our frame that hurts, but sin.

From our systems deep within   5
The crude, lashing self as king
Cracks others with a whip
Yet gives itself the slip just fine.

This self is base, unrefined,
The human so ill-defined.   10
Degrading sin is birthed,
Oozing more self and worth no good.

Murder, rape, and all theft would
Puff away like burning wood
If holy living poured   15
Through every open pore and heart.

Think of how much priceless art
Flows from righteousness, in part,
If not in whole! This world
Is not the golden pearl it was.   20

It once fell through all because
Eve, then Adam, broke God's laws
To make self boss. But Christ
Mustered heavenly might for us.

When Jesus walked, Righteousness 25
Dined with those in hopelessness.
Right living kissed the truth
As Bo'az hugged his Ruth and thrived.

Christ's cleansing blood, when He died,
Wiped away the lies I'd lied. 30
Obedience He lived,
Sin ran not through the sieve, but God.

To me, sin now seems so odd
To my spirit, soul, and bod.
Tz'dakah is the way 35
As mornings, evenings, days walk out.

DRAW NEAR

Dark bracken hid the shadowed world from view:
It shocked to realize adventures were far,
Far from what the brochures said one could do.

Cold murky pockets under mountain peaks
Bruised the back in tortured, aching slumber.　　　　5
Where was the freedom one alone could seek?

Choosing one's own journey paid a heavy
Price, so distant from home's loving shoulder.
To there ran I with feet cracked, unsteady,

Hankering, thirsty for bed—but doubtful.　　　　10
The shame to draw near thrived in shadowed fear.
"Oh son! I'm so glad you returned!," dad yelled from his castle.

SMALL & INSIGNIFICANT

None thought so much of little me;
They put me down with upraised brows,
"Not to be heard but to be seen."
To ask for love was not allowed.

They put me down with upraised brows; 5
Their rolling eyes hurt like a stab.
To ask for love was not allowed.
I gripped what my small hands could grab.

Their rolling eyes hurt like a stab,
Though later manly gaze I sought: 10
I gripped what my small hands could grab.
I found not love; much came to nought.

Though later manly gaze I sought
I wanted to be Daddy's Boy.
I found not love; much came to nought. 15
Love seemed a shallow, empty, ploy.

I wanted to be Daddy's Boy,
Then Jesus offered opened arms.
Love seemed an empty, shallow, ploy
Then Jesus offered joyful calm. 20

Then Jesus offered opened arms,
The Man from whom men hid their face!
Then Jesus offered joyful calm,
The Man who never withheld grace!

The Man from whom men hid their face 25
Outpoured His soul to bring me love.
The Man who never withheld grace
Gave significance from above.

Outpoured His soul to bring me love,
Christ crucified satanic lies! 30
Gave significance from above
My search for love has gone and died.

Christ crucified satanic lies:
No longer do I really care!
My search for love has simply died. 35
Gone is the message once declared.

No longer do I really care
None thought so much of little me.
Dead is the message once declared,
"Not to be heard but to be seen." 40

MY SHEPHERD!

The back of Classroom Four was just the spot
To traverse fields of understanding
While Mister Meagher dispensed what he had got

From years of hard-worn, hard-earned insight gained.
Interest fragmented in the back row;   5
Students flicked erasers. The shepherd strained.

I mimicked other sheep's shenanigans
Yet the unflappable English master
Expounded on how old Shakespeare began

Julius Caesar. He patiently lead   10
Me when what I deserved was the strap.
Wise knowledge and loving care put me in good stead.

LUXURIANTLY FRESH

The morning air washed fresh with scents
Perfumes my chest from floral blooms.
I ride my bike as Heaven's vents
Pass incense under stars and moons.
Gentle, it never comes too soon.   5
Then yellow wattle[3] lights the streets
And kookaburras[4] sing and croon.
Luxuriance I daily meet.

When days are done, my strength is spent;
It feels as though I am entombed.   10
I ask for restful sleep be sent
And doze within sweet Heaven's womb.
Rightful nap restores damaged plumes.
Next morning resurrection greets
When I wake to sup with my spoon.   15
Luxuriance I daily meet.

Crisp apples sweet enjoy descent
Down throats as dry as sandy dunes,
Which morning breath dried as it went
Up and down fleshly breathing tubes.   20
With life I seek to be transfused
Right through my veins from Jesus' sweet
Words of comfort He loves to use.
Luxuriance I daily meet.

---

3. *The wattle is an Australian native tree that has small, puffy, yellow blooms.*
4. *The kookaburra is an Australian bird. It is short, stocky, and squat, and when it makes its throaty calling noise, it sounds as if it is laughing.*

Envoi 25

Princes earthly do not abuse
The powers laid down at your feet.
They sap your strength, so be infused
By freshness sourced from Joy replete.

LATTICE AND SNOW

Lattice

Buttery pillars held the Temple high;
Young Solomon's triumph painted the sky,
A delightful stream where the wells ran dry.

Through church windows, coloured filters of glass
Do rainbow splendour of myriads pass: 5
Scattered hues converge like manicured grass.

The peacock bare, unfeathered, is splendid
Yet gains no prize, and remains unwedded.
Rich plumes release his beauty unfettered.

The new Temple's pillars shall have my soul 10
As lattice to decorate Heaven's poles:
My north, south, my east, and west God's might to extol.

Snow

Australia bakes to sizzle crisp and brown,
Our lips cracked where the lemon juice runs down
Burning skin broken by what the heat drowned.

Our sauna atmosphere animates flies;
Humidity smothers when down we lie   5
And wakes up the infants who scream and cry.

From eons ago on cool Nordic shores
My ancestors dwelt near Norway's fjords;
Of these sober facts I cannot ignore.

The snow and ice, and igloos of bricked strength   10
Are where I feel quite at home. White *sheleg*,
Soft powdery icing was made just for my legs.

MEDITATION & WHISPER

The stormy blackened, clapping skies torn by lightening's
Rippling, bony fingers of electric splendor
Are considered the blackboard of message Divine.

Those fingers prodded Luther's frame to repentance
And still men seek through nature's loudspeaker The Voice,   5
To hear what speaks softly in silence of stillness.

Could we withstand the naked blasts of Father's voice?
Are our ears, bones, and sinews prepared to absorb
The sonic rays of the deafening deep blue throne?

To close the eyes, visions of grandeur and comfort   10
Are seen. To silence noise, meditations of joy
Are heard. The One draped in glory whispers gently.

Discreet is the word, for though in power and might,
The Father knows that kindness is warm to our ears.
The Satan prefers the smashing, dazzling, big boast.   15

In meditation, in life slowed down, reflection
Permits the whispers of fatherly love to speak,
To restore what busyness has taken away.

The Father, Son, and Holy Spirit work as One
As long as the time is made to hear their whisper.   20
The time is short; the days are almost spent; hear now.

INSTRUCTION

The old Torah had taught me well,
A teacher strict to hold the line
Who poked me when to sleep I fell:
It came to bear each time I whined.

A teacher strict to hold the line   5
Instruction passed to make me alter;
It came to bear each time I whined,
Preparing me for Yahweh's altar.

Instruction passed to make me alter
A sacrifice to be, of course.   10
Preparing me for Yahweh's altar,
It smoothed the grains which made me coarse.

A sacrifice to be, of course,
Yes! But could Torah dissolve sin's weight?
It smoothed the grains which made me coarse;   15
For debt's release I had to wait.

Yes! But could Torah dissolve sin's weight
Who poked me when to sleep I fell?
For debt's release I had to wait.
The old Torah had taught me well.   20

TAMBOURINE

Not one to make a noise
Am I with pots or toys or things.
My family likes to sing
But the volume it brings tires me.
To live beside the sea, 5
Enjoying reverie, are mine,
To watch creation, fine,
Relaxing with sublime warm sips
Of coffee. Fingertips
Penning verse off lips of praise— 10
In these the spirit's raised,
And often amazed at what
I see about my God
In His creation, hot and cold,
Of His work humble, bold, 15
And how He breaks the mould. This means
For me the tambourine
Of praise, and on my knees His name
I honor just the same
In honest, humble frame. No ploys. 20

SUGGESTED BIBLIOGRAPHY

Now that you have read some of my own verse, perhaps you wish to explore more about poetry, and even write some of your own. Here is a very brief suggested reading list of readings on poetry:

1. Altar, Robert. *The Art of Biblical Poetry: Revised and Updated.* New York: Basic Books, 2011.

Although Altar is not a Christian, his analysis is witty and deep. He eruditely exposes the beauty of Old Testament Hebraic poetry from Scripture.

2. Drury, John, and Moul, Victoria, eds. *George Herbert: The Complete Poetry.* United Kingdom: Penguin Books, 2015.

This anthology is a well-organized collation of Herbert's poetry. Much of it concerns his own life, but he also penned profound reflections about God's creation and goodness.

3. Hamlin, Hannibal et. al., eds. *The Sidney Psalter: The Psalms of Sir Philip and Mary Sidney.* Oxford: Oxford University Press, 2009.

This anthology is a well-organized collation of Countess Pembroke's poetic interpretation of the Book of Psalms.

4. Kooser, Ted. *The Poetry Home Repair Manual: Practical Advice for Beginning Poets.* Lincoln: University of Nebraska Press, 2005.

Kooser, America's Poet Laureate from 2004–2006, has written in this small, concise book some well-seasoned advice about how to write poetry in a way that is readable, meaningful, and does not sound bombastically irritating.

5. Smith, A.J. ed. *John Donne: The Complete Poems.* London: Penguin Books, 1996.

This anthology is a well-organized collation of Donne's poetry.

6. Steele, Timothy. *All the Fun's in How You Say a Thing: An Explanation of Meter and Versification.* Athens: Ohio University Press, 1999.

Steele, an American poet who writes in meter and rhyme, lays out elaborate and systematic advice about what works, and does not work, in the writing of poetry.

www.ingramcontent.com/pod-product-compliance
Lightning Source LLC
Chambersburg PA
CBHW060430050426
42449CB00009B/2225